More Great Hymns

INTRODUCTION

This collection of some of the world's greatest hymns was created for, and is dedicated to, my good friend and musical colleague, Philip Smith, Principal Trumpet, New York Philharmonic Orchestra. The goal of these arrangements is to allow instrumentalists the opportunity to give praise and adoration to God through their musical abilities.

Though these arrangements have been written for trumpet, with Phil in mind, cued notes have been added to allow players at many different levels and on various different instruments to perform them. They are playable on all instruments (C Treble Clef, B♭ Treble Clef, E♭, F or Bass Clef) by simply purchasing the appropriate book that coincides with the key of their instrument.

The piano accompaniment book has been written to work with all instruments. An accompaniment track for each hymn is included with the online audio (which is included with all of the solo books), should a piano accompanist not be available. The audio also includes a sample performance of each arrangement with a soloist. Appropriate tuning notes have been included with the online audio to allow the soloists the opportunity to adjust their intonation to the intonation of the recorded accompaniment.

More Great Hymns is the second book in this series. The first book, *Great Hymns*, is also available through your favorite music dealer. It includes arrangements of the following hymns:

All Creatures Of Our God And King
Praise To The Lord, The Almighty
Be Thou My Vision
O Worship The King
Joyful, Joyful, We Adore Thee
Brethren, We Have Met To Worship
We Gather Together
I Sing The Mighty Power Of God
A Mighty Fortress Is Our God
All Hail The Power

May you enjoy using this collection and find it useful in extending your musical ministry.

Kindest regards,

James Curnow
President

1. HOW FIRM A FOUNDATION

Traditional
Arr. **Stephen Bulla** (ASCAP)

Piano / Organ Accompaniment

More
Great Hymns

Instrumental Solos
for Worship

Selected by James Curnow

Contents

ISBN 978-90-431-2109-5

CURNOW MUSIC

EXCLUSIVELY DISTRIBUTED BY
HAL•LEONARD®

Visit Hal Leonard Online at
www.halleonard.com

Contact us:
Hal Leonard
7777 West Bluemound Road
Milwaukee, WI 53213
Email: info@halleonard.com

In Europe, contact:
Hal Leonard Europe Limited
42 Wigmore Street
Marylebone, London, W1U 2RN
Email: info@halleonardeurope.com

In Australia, contact:
Hal Leonard Australia Pty. Ltd.
4 Lentara Court
Cheltenham, Victoria, 3192 Australia
Email: info@halleonard.com.au

More Great Hymns
Piano / Organ Accompaniment

Arranged by:
Stephen Bulla
Douglas Court
James Curnow
Timothy Johnson
Kevin Norbury

Piano / Organ Accompaniment

Piano / Organ Accompaniment

2. AMAZING GRACE

Traditional
Arr. **James Curnow** (ASCAP)

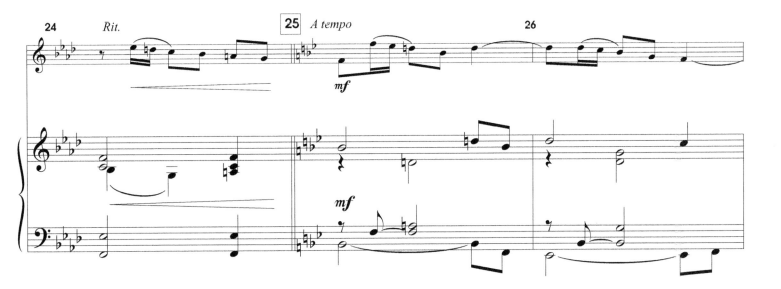

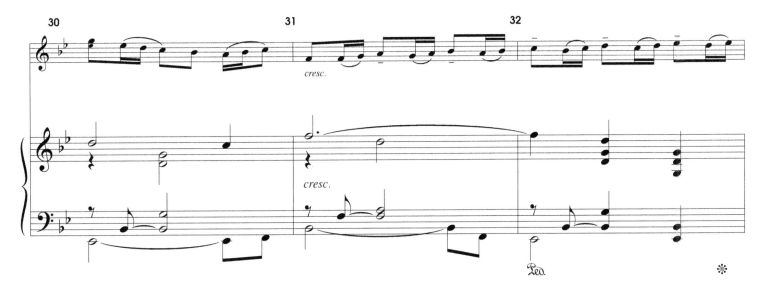

Piano / Organ Accompaniment

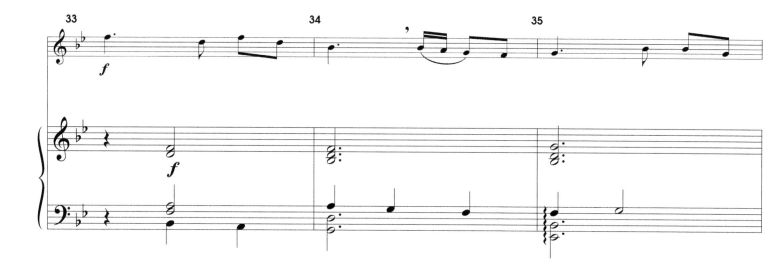

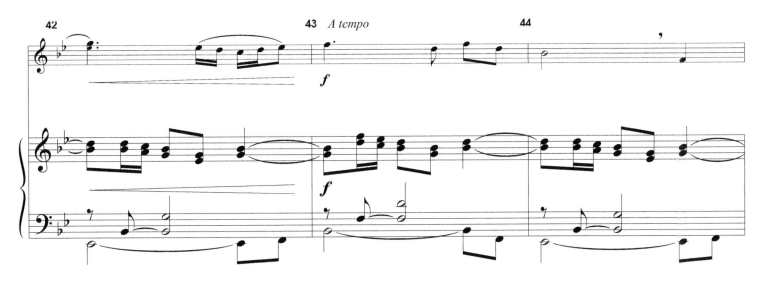

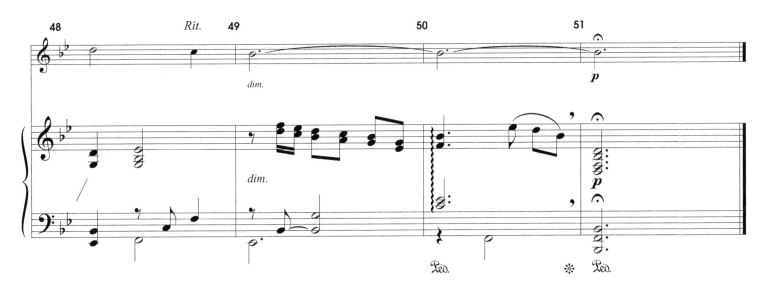

3. SOFTLY AND TENDERLY

Will L. Thompson
Arr. **Timothy Johnson** (ASCAP)

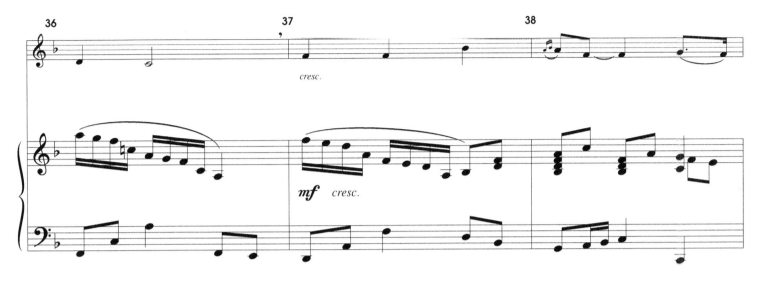

Piano / Organ Accompaniment

4. O FOR A THOUSAND TONGUES TO SING

Charles G. Glaser
Arr. **Douglas Court** (ASCAP)

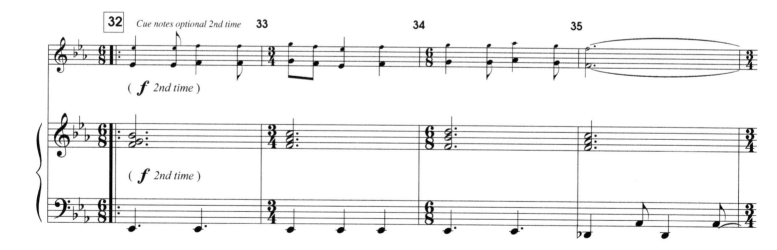

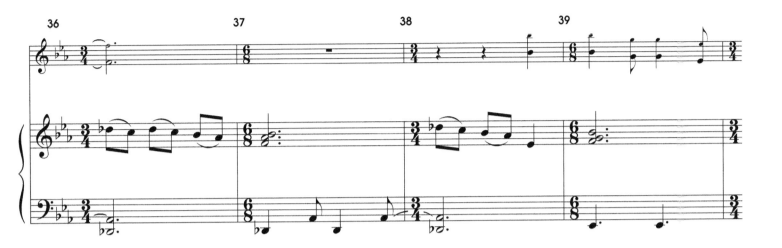

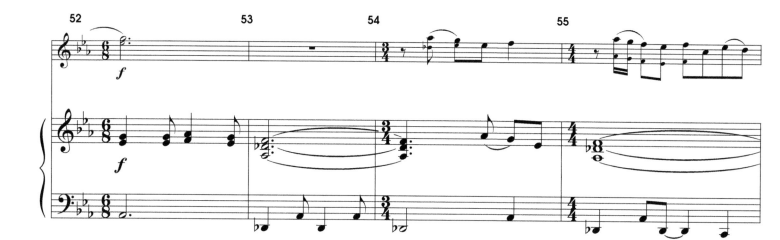

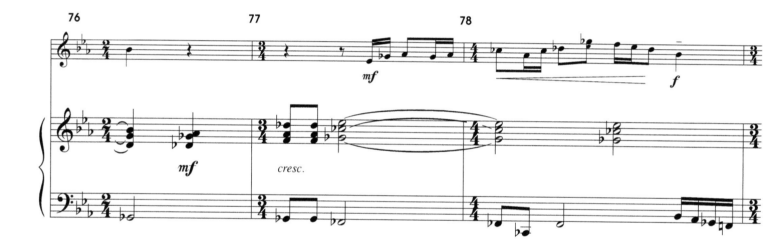

Johann Sebastian Bach
5. JESU, JOY OF MAN'S DESIRING
Arr. **Stephen Bulla** (ASCAP)

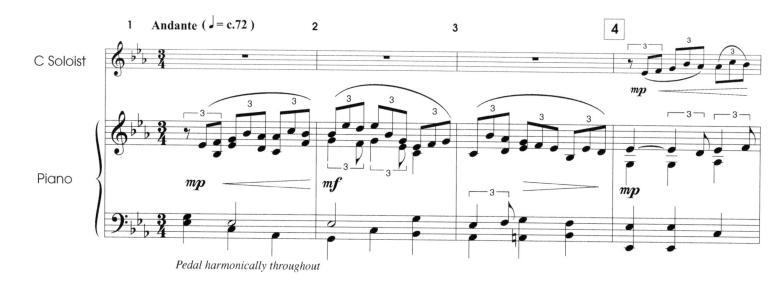

28

Piano / Organ Accompaniment

Piano / Organ Accompaniment

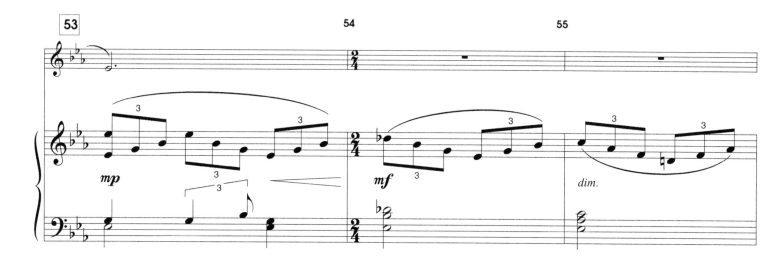

6. HOLY GOD, WE PRAISE THY NAME

From "Katholisches Gesangbuch", 1774   Arr. **Kevin Norbury** (ASCAP)

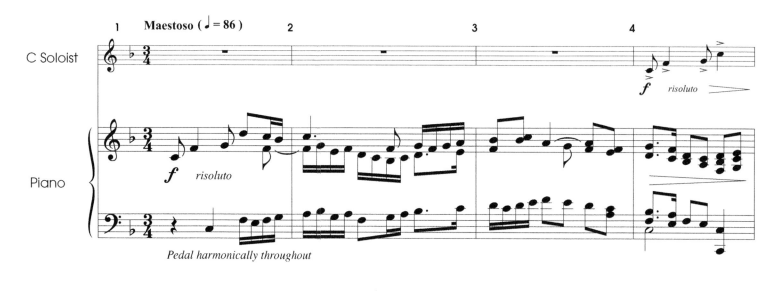

34

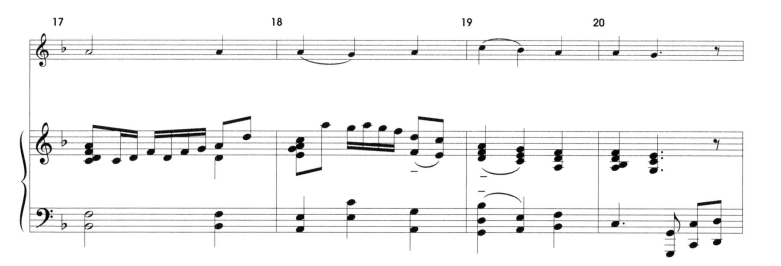

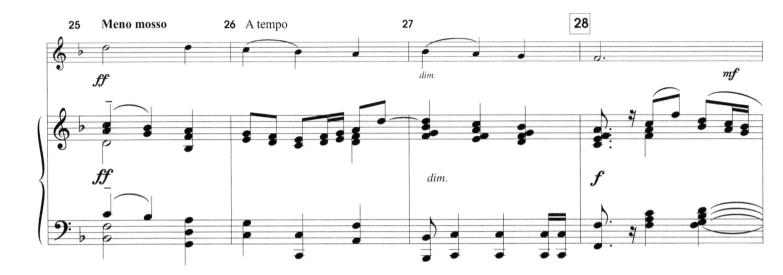

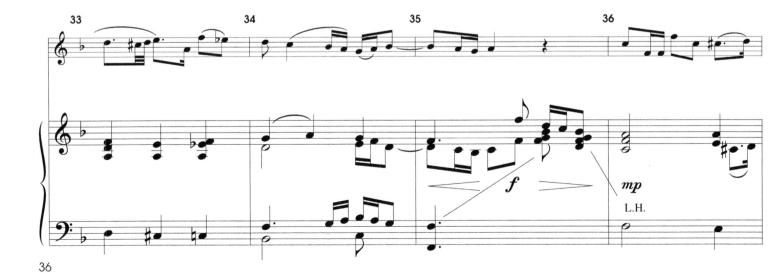

7. EASTER GLORY

Low in the Grave He Lay and Christ the Lord Is Risen Today

Robert Lowry
Charles Wesley
Arr. **James Curnow** (ASCAP)

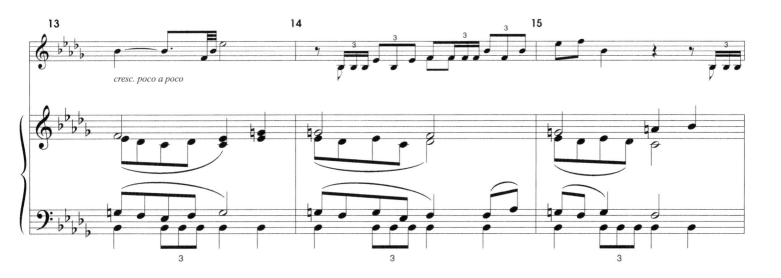

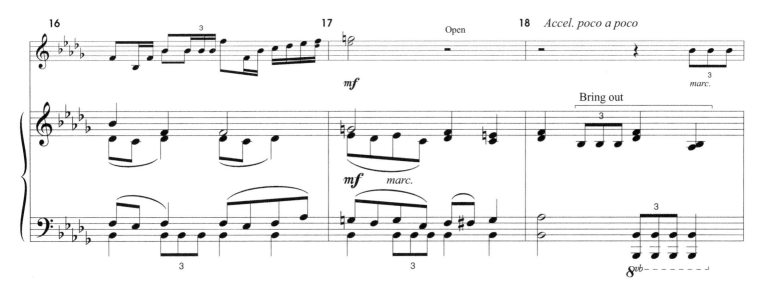

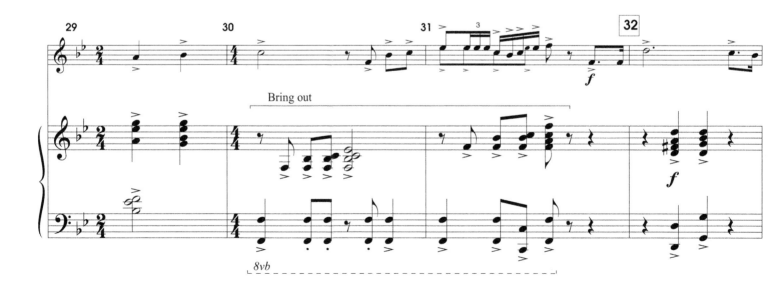

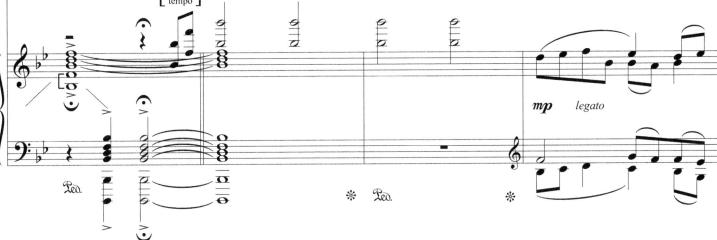

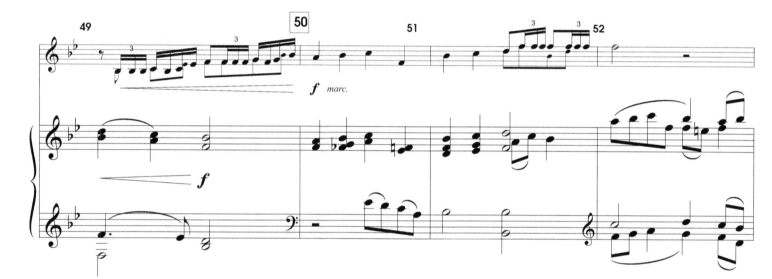

8. HOLY,HOLY,HOLY

John B. Dykes
Arr. **Douglas Court** (ASCAP)

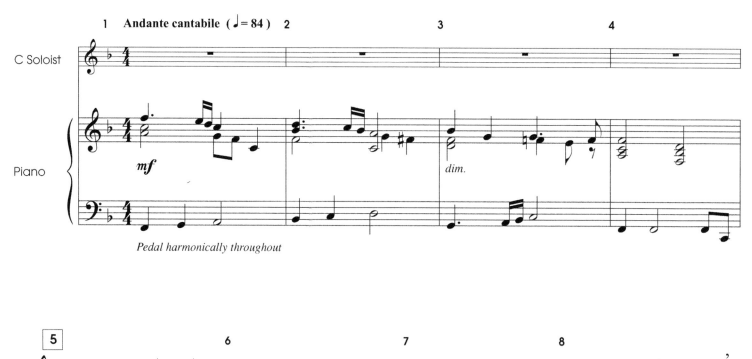

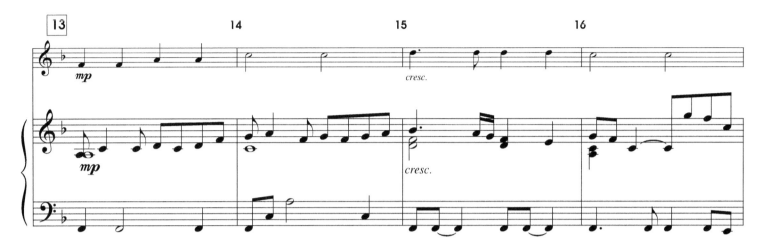

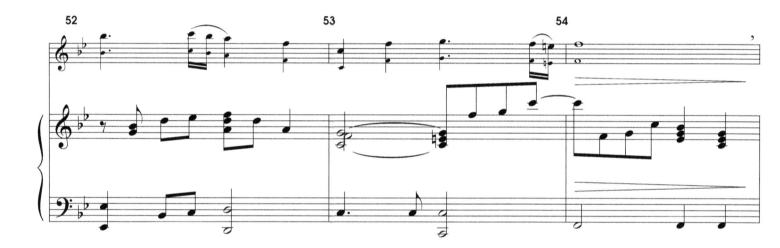

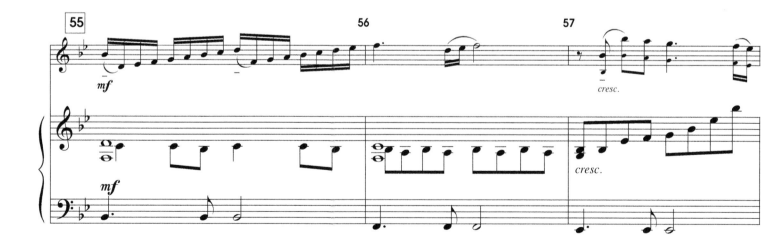

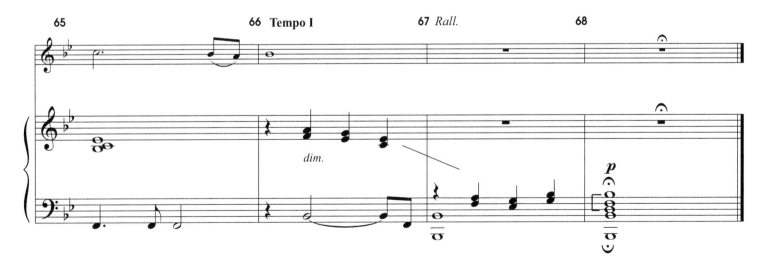

9. LEAD ON, O KING ETERNAL

Henry T. Smart
Arr. Timothy Johnson (ASCAP)

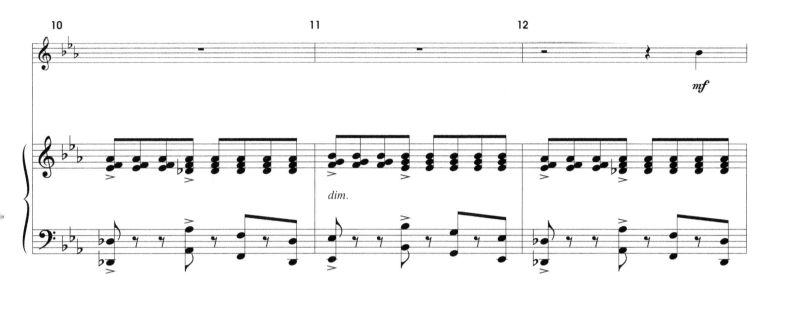

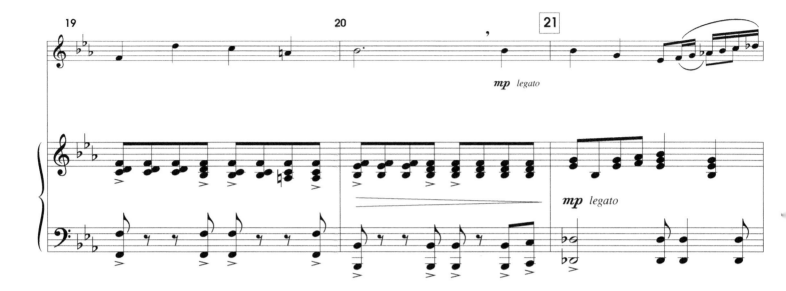

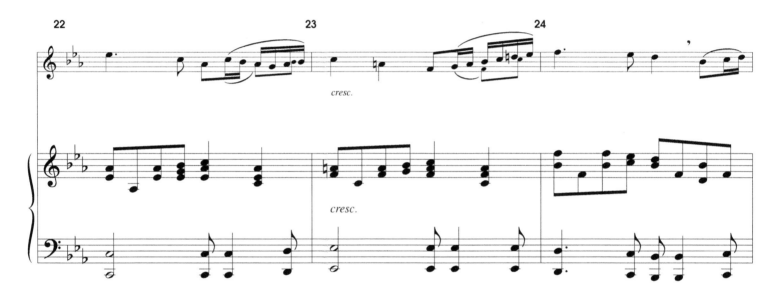

Piano / Organ Accompaniment

10. MY FAITH LOOKS UP TO THEE

Lowell Mason
Arr. **James Curnow** (ASCAP)

Piano / Organ Accompaniment

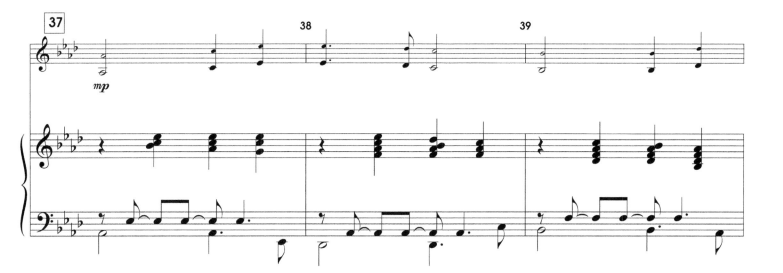

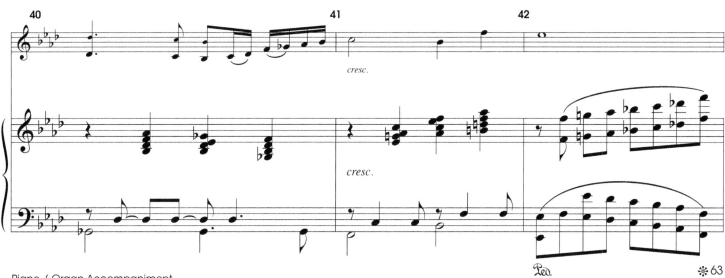

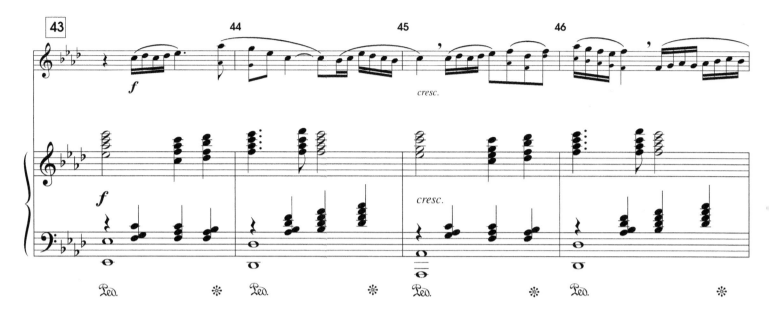

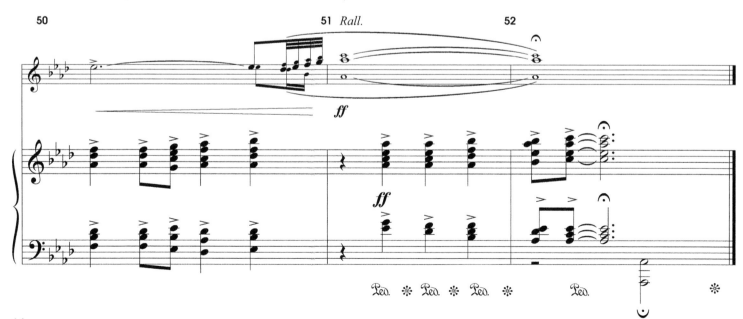